The Ultimate Guide for Rentals, Tenants and Landlords

Contents

Room Rentals in your house

Why should you rent rooms in your house? Maybe you shouldn't, but then perhaps the money would change your mind.

Room rentals? Why would you want to make your home into a boarding house? Maybe you shouldn't. I enjoyed having people living in my house, and most of them became friends. On the other hand, you might not like that arrangement. I hated being a landlord when I owned rentals that were not my home. Each of us is different.

Consider Your Room Rental Options

You don't necessarily have to live with the room-renters, so consider all the options available. You could do any of the following:

1. Rent rooms in your own home and share common space with the renters. This is what I did for several years when I was single, and it worked fine for me.

2. Partition your home so you can rent rooms without sharing common space. You'll need at least two bathrooms, and separate entrances to make this work.

3. Add an efficiency apartment for yourself, so you can have privacy, perhaps still sharing a laundry room with the renters. This is what we did when I married. It also opened up one my previous bedroom, increasing the rental income enough to pay for the new apartment in less than a year.

4. Buy a house just to rent it out by the room. This can be an excellent way to get cash flow out of homes that might not otherwise be such good investments.

5. Sublet a room in the apartment you rent. If this is okay with the landlord, it can be a way to afford a nicer apartment, or to get past financial hard times.

6. Use room rentals as a way to afford a house payment. If you are having trouble buying a home because you can't afford the payments, you can buy a home with extra rooms and rent them out.

Consider the Money in Renting Rooms

The amount you can charge for rent will vary greatly in different parts of the country. Here is what I charged renting rooms in a mobile home in a small town in northern Michigan (a few years ago):

Small Bedroom: $65 per week times 52 weeks equals $3380 per year.

Medium Bedroom: $75 per week times 52 weeks equals $3900 per year.

Large Bedroom: $85 per week times 52 weeks equals $4420 per year.

Potential Annual Income (I had a couple weeks vacancy now and then): $11,700 per year.

This was a home that I lived in, remember. I included all utilities in the rent, and I tracked my expenses closely. Including repairs to the heating system, the refrigerator and roof, as well as utilities, garbage collection, cable television, local phone service, property taxes and insurance, my costs the last year I had the house were $3,900 (I had already paid off the $253/month mortgage).

How do you figure profit when you live in the home? Renting rooms in my home probably added $300 or so to the annual costs. Heating was almost the same cost, as was garbage collection, taxes, insurance, cable television, and phone service. A little more wear and tear and a bit more electricity were the only real additional costs. In other words, almost all the extra income was profit. Or if you want to look at it another way, I lived for free and had $7800 income from the home I lived in.

Do you want to have thousands of dollars of extra income every year? What would you do with that money? Think about that, and you have the answer to why you should rent rooms.

Things to know before Buying Investment Rental Property

Rental property can be an excellent way to bring in additional money as well as invest in an asset that is actually tangible; however, investing in rental property does involve more than just purchasing a property and watching the money roll in. Many people believe that the biggest hurdle they may face is obtaining the loan; however, this may be easier than they actually think. It is other issues which you may face along the way which should be considered before you actually take the step of purchasing rental property.

First, always make sure you take the time to know exactly what you can afford. Many people make the mistake of overlooking this step, assuming that the rent will cover the mortgage payments. If you are not sure of exactly what kind of rent you can get before you purchase a property, you could find yourself in financial trouble later on. You should always research rental properties in your local area to understand the going rates for similar properties. Check the newspaper for information on going rental rates. It is also a good idea to check with your local landlord's association for rental rate information.

In addition, you need to take into consideration expenses which may come up along the way. Ideally, you should have a reserve fund established to tide you over in the event you experience emergency expenses or your property is vacant for a period of time. Before you commit to purchasing a property, make sure that you will be able to rent the property for at least an amount that will cover the mortgage as well as still have a sufficient amount left over to cover insurance premiums, maintenance costs, property taxes and income taxes.

In addition, you need to give some thought and consideration to the type of property that will best suit you. You can find rental properties in many different sizes as well as types. Each of these different types can pull in different rental rates as well as attract different types of renters. So, giving thought to the property that best suits you is really an important step which should not be overlooked.

For example, if you purchase a property that is near a college or university you are likely going to find that most, if not all, of your tenants are college students. While you may never have a vacancy, you may also find that you have a continual turnover, problems collecting rent and even possible damage to the property itself.

In addition, you should make sure you understand your responsibilities as a landlord. Keep in mind that your obligations are typically regulated by the state in which the property is located. Some states have very little regulation while other states are highly regulated. If you fail to follow state regulations you could find yourself in for quite a bit of financial as well as legal trouble. It is always best to educate yourself ahead of time.

Finally, make sure you consider how much insurance you will need to not only property the property in the event of damage or destruction but also to cover all liabilities as well. One liability claim can be enough to cause serious repercussions so this is not an issue where you want to take a short-cut. Remember that it is your responsibility as the landlord to provide liability insurance, not your tenant. If someone should slip and fall on your rental property then it will be you who is responsible, not the renter.

Rental investment property truly can be an excellent investment and income builder provided that you are prepared and understand what you should expect from the outset. Do not be afraid to seek help where you need it, especially from associations and from professionals such as attorneys. This is the hallmark that can often set a successful rental property investor apart from one who fails.

Renting a house and vacating the premises

If you plan to vacate the premises when you are renting a house, you must abide by the lease agreement. Most leases require thirty to sixty days notice that you are vacating the house. Your lease agreement will also have required time you must live in the house before the lease is expired. If you sign a one-year lease and plan to leave after the year is up, you must give proper notice. This is done in writing as well as verbal. Tell the property owner of your decision and hand him or her written letter as well.

You will still have to pay the monthly rent and clean the house you are renting to receive your security deposit back. You need to leave the house in the exact shape or better, as it was when you rented it. After you vacate the property, the property owner has thirty to sixty days to return your security deposit or a portion if it with a detailed explanation of what was wrong. If any security deposit monies are withheld, you are entitled to detailed list as to why and what it was for. If you do not receive this, you can take legal action.

Renting a house and vacating the premises requires you to turning all keys that are for the house or any other areas of the property. When doing so, you are no longer allowed to enter the house or visit the property. You should also remember to change your address and the utility bills. You should take all garbage and place it in the right area, the property owner or new renters can place it out for pick up. Never leave anything there that the property owner will have to pay to haul away, this will more than likely be ducted from your security deposit.

When vacating the premises of the house you are renting, if the property owner can rent the house out sooner than later, you may receive a prorated amount of rent to pay if you have already vacated the premises. This is always nice because you do not have pay a full month's rent at two different places. If you are required to prorate the rent, then you can take the monthly payment amount and divide by the number of days in that month. This gives you a daily amount that you times by the number of days you owe rent for on that rental.

You will also need to make sure the utilities are changed into the property owners name or the new tenants will put the utilities in their name. Never take anything for granted, ask questions to find out the right answer for what to do. Then you can give the utility companies your new address so they can send you a final bill. In addition, have the water meter read right away. Sometimes they are a little slow, which might result in a higher bill than expected when it arrives in the mail.

What questions to ask before Renting An Apartment

When you are looking at apartments, there are some questions to ask when renting an apartment. You need to know if the locks are changed. Not all property managers change the locks and count on previous owners turning in all the keys. You might want to ask for the locks to be changed, or ask if you can change them. This will protect you in the future if there are any extra keys unaccounted for by the property owner.

Another question to ask when renting an apartment is about the utility bills. You want to find out the monthly bill and if there is a budget plan, you can be on to spread out high bills during the winter months. Most property owners have this information, but if they do not, you can call the utility companies and they will tell the information for that address.

When you think about another question to ask when renting an apartment, you might forget the obvious question about grace periods for late rent. Some property owners give you a five-day grace period to pay the rent, if you go past this day, there may then be additional charges added on for late fees. You need to know this in case it would ever happen. If you are in between paychecks, you might want to save some money so you are always ahead a month.

The last question to ask when an apartment is if there are any smoke detectors in the building and are they working properly. In addition, you need to know the fire exits that are available to get out of the apartment in the event of a fire. This is very important for anyone renting or buying a home or apartment. You want to make sure there is a safe exit in case the need arises. Many people forget this question when renting an apartment or a house. You might even think of some more questions from past experiences. Ask all the questions you need to have answers for before signing any lease to ensure your peace of mind.

Some other questions to ask that most people forget about are the school district, the neighborhood reputation, if there is public transportation nearby and garbage collection schedules. These are just some more questions that people forget to ask. Another very important question would be about parking rules and regulations if you are going to park on the street. Many cities and towns that have winter weather with snow and for other reasons do not have parking on streets after a certain time.

You will want to find out this information because; you may find yourself in need of a parking place that might be farther away from your home. This could become an issue if you have to walk a good distance late at night by yourself. If you think about it, any question is a smart question when renting an apartment. You want to have something that can accommodate you and not have you accommodate it.

Things to know before signing a rental agreement

List the components of a rental agreement and how to get one that is suitable for state.

A rental agreement is a legally binding contract between the landlord and the tenant that outlines the terms and conditions of the rental.

This contract document is made up of many components. They are:-

1. The rental agreement should be very specific on the subject of abandonment. It must clearly define the landlord's options if the tenant leaves the property without notice?

2. It should outline the alterations that a tenant can make to the property. The rental agreement should clearly state the kind and extend of the alteration that is allowed or not.

3. The rental agreement should touch on the subleasing. As subleasing is very popular today, the rental agreement should state your stand very clearly on this subject to avoid future misunderstanding.

4. The rental agreement should also state very clearly what will happen in the case of defaulting on a payment. The late fees should also be outlined in the rental agreement. The tenant should know up front how much they will be penalized.

5. As a landlord you should have access to your property for inspection. The rental agreement should detail when and how you will be able to enter the property in order to inspect it, etc. State laws vary on this subject and your rental agreement should conform to the law of the state.

6. The rental agreement should state who is responsible for the maintenance of the property. If it is a joint responsibility, it should clearly state who is responsible for what.

7. Payment methods should be outlined on the rental agreement so that the tenant knows how they can pay the landlord.

8. Like maintenance, utilities are a huge part of any rental agreement. It should be clear on who will pay what bill, as well as which utilities are included in the monthly rent.

All of the above are important components to any rental agreement. In addition since state laws differ, a rental agreement can have additional clauses depending on where you are located.

The first place, and usually the best place, that you may want to search for a rental agreement is on the Internet. There are several websites that will supply you with the rental agreement form that you are looking for. One of the more reputable services is located at www.rentalagreements.net.

You have to pay a small price to purchase the rental agreement that is appropriate for your state but it is much better than drafting your own rental agreement and taking the chance of missing out on something that is crucial.

The other way to get hold of a rental agreement is to get in touch with a real estate agency. If you are lucky, they may even be able to supply you with a sample rental agreement that you can customize and use as your own.

A rental agreement is something that you must have if you are going to be renting out any property. State laws differ and your rental agreement needs to meet the laws and requirements of your state in addition to also outlining every aspect of the lease in detail.

Motor Home renting Good Vs Bad

Are you interested in renting a motor home? If you are looking to take a cross country trip or if you would like to go camping in style, but you are also on a budget, you may be in the market for a motor home rental.

If this is your first time trying to find and reserve a motor home rental, you may be unsure as to how you should proceed. Instead of heading on down to your local motor home rental station or rental company, you may want to take the time to examine motor home rentals, namely what you should look for in one. By taking the time to examine your wants, as well as your needs, you will likely find yourself traveling or camping in a motor home that is perfect for you and the rest of your group.

When looking for a motor home to rent, one of the most important factors that you should take into consideration is the cost. In the United States, you will find a large number of motor home rental companies or motor home rental stations. It is important to remember that not all rental companies or rental stations charge the same rental fees. What you will want to do is think about first comparing prices. This will prevent you from paying too much money for a motor home rental. Also, if you are on a budget, it is advised that you determine, ahead of time, how much money you have to spend on a motor home rental.

The amount of time that you will need a motor home rental for is also another important factor that you should take into consideration. Before examining for rent motor homes, you may want to speak with a motor home rental representative first. This is because, over the past few years, the popularity of motor home rentals has skyrocketed. Before getting your heart set on one particular motor home, you will want to make sure that the motor home rental of your choice is available for when you need it. It might actually be easier to walk through the lot of a motor home rental company with a representative who can give you this important information right away.

As for the choosing of a motor home rental, you will want to make sure that the motor home you rent is the right size for you and all of those who will be joining you on your next adventure. Of course, you will want to find a motor home rental that is cheap and easy to drive, but you also need to take the number of people that you will be traveling with or camping with into consideration. Motor homes are nice ways to travel and to camp, but there is nothing worse that being stuck in an overcrowded motor home.

Before agreeing to rent a motor home, you should examine the features of the motor home in question. You will want to make sure that the motor home you want to rent can provide you with everything that you need, as well as everything that you want. For instance, if you are looking to travel across the country, you may want to make sure that your motor home has a working bathroom, particularly one that includes a shower. Other features that you may want to look for in a motor home rental include a kitchen, spacious sleeping areas, an eating area, as well as a small entertainment center.

The above mentioned points are just a few of the many points that you may want to take into consideration, when looking to find a motor home rental. As a reminder, it is important that you remember that renting a motor home isn't your only option. If you would like to do so, you may want to look into buying your own motor home. With a large selection of new and used motor homes to choose from, you may very well find yourself getting a great deal on a motor home that you can call your own.

Vacation destination Rentals

Many vacationers opt to rent a home in their vacation destination rather than staying in a hotel. For these vacationers, this is a worthwhile option because it gives the vacationer a more comfortable place to stay with features such as cooking facilities which are not typically offered in commercial hotels. Finding these vacation rentals can be significantly more difficult than simply making hotel reservations but many vacationers report this to be a worthwhile effort. However, some care should be taken when renting a vacation home to ensure the quality of the home meets the expectations of the vacationers.

Finding Vacation Rentals

Finding a vacation rental property can obviously be much more difficult than simply renting a hotel during the vacation. Of course some vacationers will be lucky and have a friend or family member who owns a home in a particular vacation destination and is willing to rent it out to others. Those who do not have this type of fortunate situation have other options for finding a vacation rental property.

Many homeowners in popular vacation destinations rent out their home during the peak season. These homeowners may allow a realtor to handle the transactions. Contacting realtors in the area of the vacation destination and inquiring about available rental properties in the area is one way to start the search. The realtor will likely be able to assist you in finding a home for rent.

There are also many popular websites where homes for rent are listed directly by the owner of the home. Searching the Internet can lead you to a reliable source of homes for rent. These homes are usually divided into categories by region and will likely provide you instant access to available dates. It will likely give useful information such as whether or not pets are allowed, the number of bedrooms and bathrooms as well as the size of the home and the proximity to nearby attraction. The listing may also provide useful information regarding the furnishings of the home. Some rental properties may include items such as bedding and cookware while some may not.

Ask Questions before Renting a Vacation Home

Vacationers who wish to rent a vacation home as opposed to spending their vacation in a hotel should exercise a certain amount of caution in selecting a property to rent. Being cautious will not only enable the vacationer to ensure his rental property meets his expectations but will also help to avoid potentially dangerous situations. One way to avoid these potential problems is by asking a great deal of questions during the process.

Renting a vacation home through a rental agency is ideal for safety purposes. In these situations the agency handles the entire rental giving the renter the security of knowing they are not walking into a potentially dangerous situation. However, even in this situation the renter should ask some important questions. These questions will be explained in the subsequent paragraphs.

How old is the property? Potential renters should ask questions about the age of the property and whether or not appliances, plumbing and electricity have been updated. This is important because this type of information can mean the difference between a comfortable stay in the property and dealing with problems related to the age of the home.

What is included in the rental? While most rentals include the basic necessities, there are some rental agreements which only include the use of the house and furniture. Renters may be required to bring along bedding, towels and even cookware.

How often is the property rented and how is it maintained? These two questions are inter-related because properties which are rented often see significantly more wear and tear than properties which are only rented a couple of times per year. Properties which are rented often should employ a maid service to clean the property thoroughly between each rental and possibly during longer rental periods. What is the exact location of the property? Asking this question will enable the vacationer to determine whether or not the property is ideally situated for the purposes of the vacation.

The Renting Agreement

When trying to understand the renting agreement, you might have some difficulties if you do not understand what is being said. The first part of the renting agreement is your information as well as any other applicant who will reside in the apartment. The standard lease agreement will include abandonment of the property, repairs and alterations as well as sub-letting.

The information you supply about yourself is important for checking out your history and current working situation. If you supply wrong information, you might be denied the apartment or house. Always print your information so it is eligible, but sign your name at the bottom. The more information you supply, the better your chances are for being accepted for the rental.

The renting agreement will also include the rules of breaching the contract, drug offenses that are committed in the house and property owner access and inspection. The renting agreement will also include a clause for lawful use of the property, disclosure of lead paint, maintenance, parking, late fees and the rent. It will also verify the security deposit, hold over of the tenant, terminating and vacating the property, utilities and it will discuss surrendering the premise.

Although every state has different laws governing the specifics related to the renting agreement, it all says the same thing, just with different time frames and punishments. If you are accused and convicted of having drugs on the property, the renting agreement will state what will happen to you. This protects the property owner from possible forfeiture of the property in question.

The renting agreement discloses who is responsible for repairs and what repairs you are subject to as well as the property owner. The property owner does have a right to inspect the premises at any time with proper notification. If you read the renting agreement before signing, you will know your rights as a renter and what is expected of you while renting said property.

The renting agreement otherwise known as an apartment lease will be specific in some areas and vague in others. If you have any questions about the vague statements, ask for clarification to ensure you understand your part of the agreement. Some property owners do not fill out all the parts of an apartment lease, if you feel this needs to be filled out completely, you may want to mention that before signing anything. If you do not need that area filled out, make sure there is an X through that section so nothing can be added after you sign the agreement.

If you sign a rental agreement, make sure you receive a copy from the property owner before moving in. This will ensure that you have one to refer back to if you need clarification on anything. You should keep your rental agreement in a safe place with important papers and keep it until you receive your security deposit back after you move. This will be the only legal document you have that protects you as well as the property owner.

Unsecured loans for tenants with bad credit

Unsecured Tenant Loans, like many other unsecured loans, do not entail placing of collateral. This poses a great deal of risk for lenders with regard to repayment. Hence, Unsecured Tenant Loans have higher interest rates, shorter loan terms and a limited loan amount. On the positive side, they involve less paperwork – which means faster approval, they do not require any collateral. Unsecured Tenant Loans are typically meant for non homeowners. So, those of you who thought you had no options, start searching for your ideal Unsecured Tenant Loan today.

The "Loan World" is a complex jungle full of a variety of loans, all at your disposal. Literally – there's something for everyone! There are Personal Loans, Wedding Loans, Home Improvement Loans, Home Loans and many others. The cash obtained through these loans can then be used for home furnishing, renovation, buying that dream home/car, education or weddings. Well, what about those who have no security to offer or no collateral to put up to avail these loans? Like I said, there's something for them too, it's called an Unsecured Tenant Loan.

Being unsecured like many other loans, these Tenant Loans do not require you (the borrower) to place any collateral as security, as in case of Secured Loans. This makes Unsecured Tenant Loans very attractive to non homeowners like tenants, students, PG's, etc. However, this advantageous feature has its drawback too. Owing to the absence of collateral, lenders have to bear a greater risk with regard to repayment. With Secured Loans, in case you default on your repayments, lenders can take custody of your collateral. Conversely, in case of Unsecured Tenant Loans, defaulting on your monthly payments leaves your lenders in a lurch.

Advantages of a Tenant Loans:

·The best thing about a tenant loan is that you don't have to put any property at risk. Most people who put up their home as collateral face repossession in case of inability to repay the loan.

·Tenant Loans save your precious time in the process of procurement, as you don't have to go for valuation of property. As a result you avoid a lot of paper work.

·Tenant Loans are also available for people with bad credit histories, although the approval process is not a piece of cake.

Tenant Loans, in short, are a boon for all non homeowners like council tenants, students, etc.

From above, as you can see, as there is no collateral to consider, there obviously can be no process for valuation of collateral. This means that your Unsecured Tenant Loan will take lesser time for approval and will clearly entail lesser paperwork, making liquid cash available to you rather quickly.

Now I'm sure you're wondering why lenders offer such loans, when there's nothing in it for them. Well, here's what you've been looking for – a glitch! To explain this better, let's start talking "interest rates." To compensate for the lender's risk factor, Unsecured Tenant Loans come with fairly high rates of interest. In addition to this, lenders need to make sure that the Unsecured Tenant Loans are repaid as soon as possible and so these loans have relatively short loan terms. As a precaution, the loan amounts are also restricted or limited as compared to Secured Loans. For example: For basic secured loans, the loan amount ranges from £5,000 to $75,000 and the repayment period extends from 5 to 25 years. While for Unsecured Tenant Loans, lenders tend to limit the value to $25,000 and the loan term extends up to 10 years only. So nothing can be perfect after all!

Disadvantages of Tenant Loans:

·   Tenant Loans come with high interest rates because of the absence of collateral.

·   The loan terms of Tenant Loans are very short to facilitate quick repayment.

·   Tenant Loans grant only small loan amounts for the same reasons.

Unsecured Tenant Loans lenders too, are businessmen after all and have to have a reason for granting you your loan. For this, besides considering loan amount, loan terms and interest rates they need to mull over your repayment capability. They can gauge your repayment potential after checking on your credit history and financial standing. A good credit history will further accelerate the approval procedure while a bad credit history will slow down the process. Here, please remember, that bad credit doesn't necessarily stop you from getting your Unsecured Tenant Loan. Even those of you with bad credit due to a past bankruptcy, default in repayments, C.C. J's (County Court Judgments) or arrears stand a fair chance of getting an Unsecured Tenant Loan approved.

Every Unsecured Tenant Loan is tailored to your needs and financial standing, so choose wisely. You must have extensive knowledge about current rates and options to finalize any loan. Take expert advice from knowledgeable people. Getting as many quotes from as many Unsecured Tenant Loan lenders as possible simplifies the situation.

… Like I said earlier, "There's something for everyone." So get going today!

Free Money for Teenager's

Unsecured loans for tenant do not involve any sort of collateral. Sufficient amount is disposed with this scheme at considerable rate of interest and comfortable repayment tenure. This loan is easy to get and also the processing time it takes is very less.

Obtaining a loan in present scenario is a cakewalk to homeowners but things get a bit murkier for tenants to attain usual loans. To ease them and extract the customer base inclusive of tenants, unsecured loans for tenant have been designed. These loans serve one with cash when he is stung by the deficiency of the same.

Features and uses of loan

Tenant can use this loan for various purposes like purchasing a brand new car or bike, going for an exotic holiday, consolidating debt, buying a new flat or apartment, expenses in your dear ones wedding, etc. As stated earlier unsecured loans for tenants fall under category of unsecured loan, so you need not have to put anything as collateral here. But as lender is at higher risk, the rate of interest is slightly high also the repayment period is shorter. You can procure an amount varying from£500 to £2500.Having a good credit history will help you obtain higher amount. The interest rate lies somewhere between 7.7% APR to 18.3%.Being informed and good groundwork like visiting various lenders will definitely help you in negotiations.

Eligibility and availability

Any type of tenant can apply for this kind of loan. You may be Council tenants, Private tenants, housing association tenants, or even tenants living with parents. In order to get loan you must also fulfill these criteria: you should be in salaried employment presently when yon you go for obtaining loan, You must have resided at your current address for over 12 months, You should have your personal U.K. bank account, having a credit/store card, You have a savings account to which you make regular payments. You can apply for this kind of loan to traditional money lenders or bank, or else you can apply online. Applying online saves your time and it also consumes less processing time. So just fill some simple forms and you have applied for loan.

Complex jungle tenant loans

Now payday loan lenders offering unsecured loans for tenants. These loans have convenient approval process especially for bad credit holder tenants. For getting these loans borrower must have a live bank account and he must be above 18 years salaried citizen of UK. You just fill a simple online form and get $250- $25,000 on affordable rates of interest without collateral within 24 hours of applying.

Payday loan lenders now offering loans design especially for tenants. Now the people those are not a homeowner can also get the cash loan without any security and hassle. http://www.unsecuredloansfortenants.com unsecured loans for tenants have a convenient loan approval process for tenants.

If you are a tenant of local councils, housing associations or other similar government landlords, then there are lenders who offer unsecured loans for you whether you have bad credit, default, arrears or CCJ. Lenders have no problem because of your bad credit history.

Requirements for these loans are that you should be

- An UK citizen with age of above 18 years.

- A salaried person and get monthly income up to $1000.

- You must have an active checking account in any reputed bank of UK.

If you fulfill these requirements then you can easily get these loans without any hassle and inconvenience. Just visit to the website and fill a simple form within 5 minute you get approval and then within 24 hours you get the loan amount directly in your checking account.

The main features of these loans are that you can borrow the amount between £250 and £25,000, its rate of interest to be charged depends on loan amount, it suits the tenants those have no home to keep as collateral because it is an unsecured loan, its services are free and easily available by the help of internet, flexibility of terms, repayment terms are made according to your pocket. So, the tenants who need money have no need to visit any where for money we will arrange the cash as soon as possible.

Landlords Renting Out

In the advent of the subprime mortgage crisis many homeowners are opting to rent properties as opposed to trying to sell in this unstable and already saturated market. But, land lording involves some savvy, so listen up and heed some valuable advice, before diving into the world of renting and leasing your home.

In the advent of the subprime mortgage crisis many homeowners are opting to rent properties as opposed to trying to sell in this unstable and already saturated market. But, land lording involves some savvy, so listen up and heed some valuable advice, before diving into the world of renting and leasing your home.

Number one, take note that you're not the only one is this position, so don't immediately assume it'll be easy as pie and that you'll fetch a pretty penny in terms of your rental income. The reality is that in 2005 and 2006 when money flowed like Italian table wine, well everyone had the same idea to get rich fast through real estate. Today, these folks are your competitor landlords and it's dog eat dog out there. With all this competition, there's a lot on the market and rental prices are being driven steadily downward.

Because of this competitive market, if you want to ensure your place gets rented and stays rented for a while, then you're going to have to price right- and in most cases this means under pricing your rental property. So keep a close eye on similar rentals in your area and be prepared to bite the bullet and offer yours at a bit less than everyone else's. You want to be the dog with the bone, right? So, jump through the right hoops Bo Bo...

Make sure you meet your prospective tenants and do a proper walk-though with them to take stock on the condition of the property and to go over the terms of the lease. Of course, you'll also want to check up on their credentials and credit history. Be absolutely thorough with this. Ask for references, both professional and personal and then call those references. You'll want to use your instinct as well- but some hard and fast research is necessary to ensure these new tenants will be good custodians of your property.

When contemplating the idea of renting you must understand that there are still costs associated with renting a property. In many cases you won't always be able to charge as much as your monthly mortgage payments, so be prepared for that shocker. Also factor in maintenance fees, insurance, the cost to make ready and to clean-up/repair when the tenant moves out. Likewise, if you use a rental agency this is another substantial cost to factor in. At the end of the day, you'll want to compare these costs with the cost of selling your home and decide whether or not it's actually worth it to rent.

Renting out A Home in today's market

If you plan to rent a home, you need to know some tips for renting a home as to what you can and cannot do. You will need permission from the property owner before you make any cosmetic changes to the home. If you want to paint the walls or change the look of the woodwork, you will want to obtain permission. If you do not have permission from the property owner, you could be in violation of the lease agreement.

If you have a yard, you can pretty much make this as beautiful as you want, but you cannot let the property go without proper care. Whatever the stipulations are for the yard and care need to be respected. If you are renting a home, always ask the owner how they expect the yard to look and what they expect from you. By finding out more information, you and the property owner will get along better.

If the home has a pool or any other outside recreational equipment, you need to know how to take care of the equipment and keep it in good working order. Renting a home with kids and a pool will require even more attention. You will want to keep the kids away from the water when you are not around, this may require putting up a fence around the pool and the owner will have to okay this first. Some owners will find this unacceptable, so this might not be a good place for to rent.

There are many tips for renting a home, you might think about different tips as you begin to look for homes. Not everyone will know exactly what he or she wants or needs until they find it. Sometimes you will find a home that is just what you have been looking for without even knowing it. Even if you find a home or apartment you like, you should fill out the rental application, but maybe look at a few more places to make sure. This just helps you reassure yourself that you have found what you are looking for in a rental unit.

If you need a home with so many bedrooms or you need a place that has a handicap accessible ramp for a wheelchair, you will have to discuss alterations with the property owner. For the most part, ramps are going to be at your expense and if a property owner likes your application and references, you will more than likely be able to accommodate a wheelchair if there is enough room required by the housing authority.

If you need things changed in the house itself, this might be an expense that the property owner may not want to share. This could result in you paying for something out of your own pocket for a rental that only benefits you as long as you live there. You should always talk to a potential property owner about your needs if they are not something that occurs every day for them.

Avoiding Problem Tenants

Having the right tenants in your property can truly make a huge difference in your ability to succeed in owning investment rental property. While problem renters can definitely exhibit some warning signs, there are some problem renters who are quite adept at getting past landlords. As a result, it is important to understand that you simply cannot always rely on your first impression of a prospective tenant in order to determine whether they will be responsible and reliable.

There are some tips you can use; however, in order to avoid tenants which could prove to be difficult.

First, always have prospective tenants complete a rental application. The application should be in writing and should provide you with the information you need to make a decision regarding renting the property. Along those lines; however, you need to make sure that you always follow laws, such as the Fair Housing Act. Discriminating against prospective renters is against the law and could land you in quite a bit of trouble. You are not allowed to deny someone the ability to rent your property based on religion, race, etc. By following the Fair Housing Act, you can make sure that you do not violate any discrimination laws.

Always make sure that you obtain proof of identity. This includes seeing photo identification from any prospective tenants that you interview. On the rental application you have prospective tenants complete, make sure they write down their driver license information. Make a copy of the photo ID and be certain that you attach it to the rental application.

Many landlords make the mistake of not performing a background check. This is a mistake that you cannot afford to make if you want to ensure that you avoid potentially troublesome tenants. Performing a background check gives you the opportunity to determine if there are any previous problems. For example, running a background check can let you know if a prospective tenant has a history of destroying property or skipping out on the rent.

Along with a background check, you should also perform a credit check. You will need to obtain the applicant's permission in order to do this; however, you can do this on the rental application. You will also need to obtain the applicant's Social Security number on the application to run a credit check.

References are also essential. Make sure that you obtain the name of the applicant's previous landlord so you can follow-up. This is because not all landlords make a report to the authorities when there is a problem, so by checking with the landlord directly you have a better chance of determining if there were any problems.

In addition, ask for character references. Make sure that you take the time to actually check with those references. If the applicant did not give you a valid reference this is a good way to find out about it and weed out the applicant.

Finally, make sure that you include information regarding a code of conduct with each application or lease. The code of contact should state what is expected of the tenant and have the prospective tenant sign and date the document. By making sure that these expectations are clearly outlined in the beginning, you can help to avoid a number of problems.

Downfalls in Owning Investment Rental Property

Owning and operating investment rental property can provide a number of important advantages. There are potential disadvantages to owning rental property; however, you can help to minimize possible pitfalls by following certain guidelines to protect your investment.

First, always make sure that your expectations regarding investing in rental property are reasonable and realistic. You should always approach the investment of rental property with the goal of achieving a positive cash flow; however, do not expect that you will be able to buy a new vacation home within a year.

In addition, it is important to make sure that you take the time to do your research and ensure that you understand the rules and regulations regarding the ownership and operation of rental property. As the owner of rental property, you must abide by certain federal and state laws which provide specific information regarding your liabilities and responsibilities.

Along those same lines, it is important to be certain that any lease or rental agreements you handle are absolutely legal. If you handle a lease or rental agreement which is not legal, you may experience a number of problems if your tenant happens to violate terms of the lease. To be safe, it is best to have an attorney draft your lease and rental agreements.

Before purchasing any rental property, be sure to have the property inspected or else you may discover you are facing a set of expenses you did not anticipate. Having the property inspected by a professional before you sign on the dotted line will involve an expense; however, compared to the expenses you could face by purchasing a property without an inspection, it is certainly well worth it.

When you begin the process of renting out your property, take the time to run credit checks and call references. These are both steps which many novice landlords often overlook in their rush to fill their rental properties and begin turning a profit; however, it can be detrimental. Remember that having an empty unit is always better than rushing and having an irresponsible tenant who may destroy your property, get behind on their rent and ultimately prove difficult to evict.

Joining the Landlords' Association in your local area can also prove to be helpful by putting you in connection with experienced investors and landlords. You can also gain access to reliable contractors, inspectors and other professionals who can make the process of operating rental property much easier.

It is also imperative that you make sure you have adequate property insurance as well as liability insurance. Property insurance will help to protect your investment while liability insurance will protect you in the event anything should happen to someone while on your property.

Finally, make sure you take the time to establish an emergency fund in order to cover expenses which may crop up unexpectedly. Remember that you are operating a business and as such you must be prepared for those times when expenses arise. The exact amount that you wish to contribute to your emergency fund is ultimately up to you; however, it should be sufficient to cover typical expenses that may arise. The general rule of thumb is to put aside 20% of the value of your property. To make the process of establishing an emergency fund easier, consider setting aside a certain amount of your rental receipts each month into a special account.

Important decision when Locating the Right Rental Property

The decision to invest in rental property is an important one. The first step in getting started is to choose the right property which will generate a sufficient amount of income for you while also requiring as little maintenance and upkeep as possible.

Ideally, it is best to develop a list which you can take with you when you begin the process of shopping around for the right rental property. This list will help to keep you on track and focused on what you should look for as well as what you should steer away from.

When looking for the right rental property, you will want to take several factors into consideration.

First, you should always consider the condition of the property. Generally, it is best to keep in mind that if you come across a property with a price that seems too good to be true, there is usually a reason why the property is priced so low. Many real estate investors like to point out the fact that you are able to determine your profit when you purchase a property.

While you may not consider selling the property for some time and will instead be renting it out, it is still important to take into consideration the cost of any necessary renovations and repairs before you make a final decision regarding whether you will purchase the property or not. After considering these factors, you may find that it will actually be less expensive to purchase a property that is in better condition, although at a higher price, than to purchase a property with a lower price that requires extensive renovations and repairs to get it ready to rent out.

Location is, of course, one of the essential elements of purchasing the right rental property as well. Keep in mind that properties which are located directly on a busy street may not be appealing to tenants who like a quiet and peaceful neighborhood. On the other hand, a property which is located near schools or parks will likely be more appealing to families.

It is also important to find out the history on the property and specifically whether the property has ever been used as a rental property. This is important due to the fact that in some cases a property can get a bad reputation. It does not take long for word to get around and once that occurs it can be difficult to get past it.

If the property is currently being used as a rental property, you also need to consider whether tenants are already on the property. If that is the case then you may need to honor the current lease with those tenants. This means that you may not be able to raise the rent until the lease has expired. There may even be state laws in some cases which could regulate how much you are able to raise the rent. Obviously, this is something that should be carefully considered. While there is the obvious advantage of already having tenants on the property, you may find later that this is actually somewhat of a bit of a disadvantage so be sure to carefully consider this factor.

Maintenance and repair needs of the property should also be taken into consideration. In the event that you are not able to maintain the property or repair it, this will translate to hiring a property manager and/or repair person. This means extra expenses which will reduce your profits. Of course, it also gives you some free time so you will have to weigh the advantages and disadvantages.

Finally, consider the price of the property. You always need to make sure that you will be able to cover not only the mortgage payment, if you have one, but also other expenses such as taxes and insurance. In the event the property is not occupied for a period of time, you will still need to meet all of those expenses so be certain that you can cover them before you obligate yourself.

Vacancies in your Rental Property....What to do

From time to time you will have vacancies in your investment rental property. When that occurs, you will naturally want to rent the property as quickly as possible so that you do not lose out on any rent money. It could even be that when you purchase the property, it could be vacant. There could be many reasons why it could potentially take some time to find tenants. Perhaps the location is affecting it. Or, it could be that there are simply a number of properties for rent in the local area. Regardless of why your property is vacant you will need to get it rented as quickly as possible.

For every month that your property is vacant, you are losing money in revenue. There are some things you can do to reduce the amount of time that your property is vacant; however.

First, when your property is vacant, use that time to your advantage by making any repairs that are necessary and handling any maintenance tasks. In addition, you might also consider doing something to make the property more appealing such as touching up the paint or sprucing up the yard.

You might also consider providing some type of incentive or discount in order to get your property rented more quickly. Certainly this will cost a bit of money but in the long run it is often less expensive to provide an incentive in order to get your property rented more quickly than to allow it to sit vacant for a period of time. You might think about reducing the rent or installing something in the apartment that would be appealing to prospective tenants such as a washer and dryer.

Make sure you making strong efforts to market your rental property but running ads in all of the local papers and hanging up flyers at places of interest. Of course, you should also have a For Rent sign posted on the property so that everyone who drives by will see it and know the property is available for rent or lease. Once again, a small amount of money spent on marketing is less expensive than the amount of lost revenue you could incur by allowing the property to sit vacant.

In addition, take be proactive and begin the search for tenants before your current tenant moves out if you have reason to believe that they will be leaving soon. It is never a good idea to wait until the last minute and then try to fill a vacancy. You might even ask the current tenants if they know of anyone who might be interested in renting the property. It could be quite possible that they have friends who have visited and would jump at the chance to rent the property once it is available.

Keep in mind; however, that as important as it is to rent your property quickly and avoid a vacancy you also do not want to rent out the property so quickly that you fail to conduct a thorough screening. The first time you receive an inquiry on the property, you need to begin the screening process. Take the time to obtain some basic preliminary information about applicants while also providing information about your rental property.

Of course, you must abide by fair housing laws and you also must make sure you are fair in asking the same questions of all applicants so it is a good idea to write down your pre-qualifying questions so you can be sure that you are being fair. If you are unsure of what you are allowed and not allowed to ask by law, consider consulting an attorney.

Before you end the phone call with the applicant, encourage them to drive by the property so they can see it in person and then call to make an appointment with you to see the interior.

Finding a Rental Apartment...... Comparison Shopping

Finding a rental apartment is not always easy. Depending on occupancy rates in a particular area, it actually might be quite difficult to find available apartments that are also within your price range and meet all of your pre-determined requirements. However, even in areas where there is not a great deal of competition for the available apartments, renters may still have some difficulty finding the perfect apartment. This article will offer some tips for finding a rental apartment that suits all of your needs.

Figure Out Your Needs

The first step of any apartment search should begin with the potential renter carefully identifying all of their needs in an apartment. This list of needs will be different for every renter. While some renters are simply looking for a place to eat, bathe and sleep other renters may be looking for a living space which will serve a number of purposes including working, entertaining and participating in leisure activities or hobbies. When making this list of needs the renter should consider the options they cannot live without as well as the options they want to have but can live without. It is important to make this distinction because the renter will want to ensure the apartment they choose has all of the features they need and ideally a few features they want. However, an apartment which does not have all the required features may become an uncomfortable living situation very quickly.

Do Your Research

Once a renter has a good idea of the basic features he is looking for in an apartment, he should begin researching his options. Researching apartments can be done on the Internet, through the newspaper or through rental magazines. Renters may use one of these research methods exclusively or may combine a few of the methods to form a customized strategy for researching apartments. The research phase will give the renter an idea of the types of properties available for rent in the area.

Comparison Shop

The next step is the process of comparison shopping. This basically entails visiting several different rental properties and touring these facilities. During the tour the renter will get a good idea of available options as well as the costs associated with these options. This is helpful for two very important reasons. First it gives the renter a good idea of the types of apartments available within their budget. Second it gives the renter the ability to bargain regarding price. Renters who have proof of other apartment complexes offering more favorable rental terms, may be able to entice another complex to lower their prices slightly.

Ask for Recommendations

Renters can also help themselves in their search for an apartment by seeking recommendations from trusted friends and family members. These recommendations can be taken to be much more worthwhile than recommendations offered by the apartment complex from previously satisfied tenants. It is important to note the apartment complex is likely to only offer testimony from tenants who were happy with their rental agreement. For this reason, opinions offered by friends and family members are much more valuable because they do not have a vested interest in the rental property and simply offer their honest opinion. Friends or family members who share your interests and personality traits can be very helpful in offering recommendations for apartments because it is very likely you will be happy with the apartment they recommend.

Consult the Better Business Bureau

Finally, renters should consult the Better Business Bureau (BBB) before making a final decision and choosing an apartment complex. This can be very helpful especially if the renter finds a particular apartment complex has a number of unresolved complaints against them. While a lack of complaints is not necessarily an endorsement, it is a good sign if the complex has been in business for number of years without a slew of unresolved complaints.

Loud Tenants

One of the most common issues that many landlords must deal with when they have investment rental property is music. It is not uncommon for many renters to either play music quite loud or play an instrument. This can be disturbing to neighbors and as a result you may receive phone calls of complaint. How you handle these issues is quite important because it involves a fine balance of maintaining happy renters and yet ensuring that neighbors surrounding your property are not disturbed.

In the event that you own a multi-dwelling property this can be even more of an important issue as other tenants in the building may not appreciate being disturbed by loud music. If you fail to handle the issue properly they may decide to rent elsewhere; leaving you with vacancies and that can be expensive. Furthermore, your property may gain a bad reputation, making it difficult to rent to future tenants as well.

When you are facing this type or problem there are actually several different ways that you can handle the issue. First, it is imperative that you make sure you have discussed your property rules with tenants before they actually move in. This type of action can help to prevent problems before they even begin.

Ensure that you have included terms within your lease stating when exactly music may be played. You should also include in your lease statements indicating specific times when music may not be played so loudly that it can be heard outside the individual unit. For example, you might state that music may not be played before 8am and after 10pm. You should also make sure that these terms include not only music but also actual musical instruments as well as televisions.

In addition, make sure you check on your property periodically to ensure that your tenants are not playing loud music at night or early in the morning. If you find that they are breaking this rule, do not hesitate to let them know that they are violating the terms of their lease. If you allow the issue to continue unchecked you are sending the message that this behavior is acceptable to you and later on it could be quite difficult to stop when the complaints begin rolling in.

Sometimes, checking on a property early in the morning or late at night is not feasible; especially if you live a good distance away. In this case, consider asking your neighbors to advise you if your tenants disturb them with loud music or noise. Remember that it is always best for neighbors in the area to advise you about the problem so that you will have an opportunity to correct it before they contact the city or the police with their complaints. This will also assure neighbors that you are concerned about the neighborhood and maintaining a peaceful atmosphere for everyone.

Once you have contacted your tenant verbally regarding the matter, make sure you follow-up with a reminder in writing. This should help your tenant(s) to understand the severity of the situation and will also provide you with the documentation you need in the event the behavior continues and you must consider evicting them because of it.

Ideally, the best way to handle this type of situation is to prevent it before it ever begins. Explain to your tenants when they move in that you regard the issue as serious and that you will check up on the property from time to time. If you decide to rent to students, this is especially important. By making sure that you have established a cordial relationship with your tenants early on they will be far more likely to respect your rules and understand where the line is drawn so they will not cross it.

Properly managing a rental property means not only providing a pleasant living environment for your tenants but also ensuring that your rental property does not disturb others in the neighborhood.

Turning a profit as a Successful Landlord

The ultimate goal of investing in rental property is turn a profit. To make sure that you achieve that goal it is essential that you follow several critical guidelines.

First, always make sure that you check references. This can be a burdensome step that many landlords overlook if they feel as though they have a good instinct about the tenant when they meet with them. Not checking references; however, can lead to a number of problems. You can uncover a wealth of information about potential problems before you rent to a prospective tenant.

Always make sure that you have everything in writing. This is to protect not only your rights but also the rights of your tenants as well. Everything from the code of conduct you expect tenants to abide by while renting your property to the rental application itself should be in writing.

You will find that you have better success with your rental property if you take the time to ensure that it is both secure and clean. The grounds of the property should be free of clear and trimmed regularly. Not only will the property be more visually appealing but these actions will also assist you with property liability. You will also want to take additional security measures. Extra security may be able to lower your insurance premiums as well as provide an incentive to quality tenants to rent your property when they know it is secure.

If you make the decision to hire a property manager, take the time to interview prospective candidates very carefully. Property managers can be quite helpful if you do not have the time to tend to all of the details yourself. The wrong property manager; however, can cause you tremendous problems. This means that you will need to hire a thoroughly responsible and professional individual to handle the job. Always make sure that you obtain adequate insurance. Not only should you have property insurance but you should also have liability insurance. One incident is all it takes to wipe out your investment. Check with your state to determine if any additional insurance coverage is required.

Regardless of the condition the property was in when you purchased it, there will come a time when repairs are needed. This is part and parcel of owning rental property. If you take too long to make repairs, not only will your property suffer and repairs will ultimately cost more to take care of but you will also likely lose quality tenants as well. By making sure that you handle repairs promptly you will be able to maintain the life of your property as well as retain good tenants.

Always make sure that you follow all applicable regulations in the renting of your investment property. The Fair Housing Administration Act provides precise regulations in order to prevent discrimination. If you violate those regulations you could find yourself facing a lawsuit that is costly in terms of time as well as money. The best course of action is to take the time to do your homework and consult an attorney experienced in real estate matters for guidance regarding the FHA as well as ensuring that you have the proper forms.

Finally, make sure that you do not violate the privacy of your tenants. Check with your state's regulations to find out whether you must provide any type of notice to your tenant before you enter the dwelling.

Following these guidelines will help you to retain quality tenants and avoid any potential legal problems.

Renting with pets

When you are looking for a place to rent and you have a dog or a cat, you may find the apartments available are few and in between. Many property owners today do not want to rent their properties to owners of pets. The reason is because of bad experiences in the past, or they do not like pets. If this is the situation, you may have a hard time finding a place where your pets will be welcomed. If you do find a place that will allow renting with pets, you may have to pay an extra pet deposit or even a higher monthly rent.

If you are renting with pets, and decide after a while, you do not want pets anymore, you want to have a clause in your rental agreement that will lower the rent if you are paying extra or that the property owner can inspect the place and return your pet deposit. The property owner and you as the renter should agree to this prior to signing the rental agreement. You do not want to have monies held for a pet you do no longer have in the apartment or house.

Renting with pets is sometimes the hardest thing to accomplish. You may find that places that allow pets are not as nice as a place that does not allow pets. You should always look at many places rather than just a few before making a decision. Another issue with renting with pets is that you may find the apartment or house that previously had pets, attracts bad behavior from your pets. There is one sure way to find out if there are pet urines spots that could attract your pets to follow suit.

Property owners can do this before returning pet deposits as well. Take a black light and go over carpets, walls and hardwood flooring to see if there is evidence of pet urine. This works well for finding out if there could be potential problems with your pets. If you do find areas with urine, you should point these out to the property owner before your pet enters the rental unit.

You are going to find that most property owners will not accept pets. There are some however, that do but you need to know how to present your pet. If you have a dog, it is a good idea to explain the age, how long you have had the dog and if it has any behavior problems. Property owners also look at the type of dog you have because many homeowner insurance policies will not provide insurance if you have a certain breed of dog. This will be a deciding fact for property owners even if they allow pets.

If you have a fish aquarium or a small rodent such as a hamster, it may not be a problem with a property owner. You just have to learn how to present your pet in a way that is flattering and not negative.

Things to know and look for Before Renting A Home

There are some things to check on before renting a home. The first thing to check is the average utility bills. You can find this information by calling the utility company and requesting a printout of the last year's monthly charges. This will give you an idea of what the monthly charges would be for you as well. Renting a home with new windows, doors and insulation will provide lower utility bills, therefore, you should always find out if the home is insulated and check the windows for seals.

You should always check the basement for leaks as well as termite tunnels. Many property owners do not know about the conditions in the basement because they pay more attention to the living quarters. You will want make sure there are hook ups for the washer and dryer, a drain and check the pipes to make sure they are in good condition. The stairs should be in good conditions as well as have a hand railing. Many property owners have no idea what conditions the stairs or railing are in when they are renting a place.

Other things to look for when renting a house are the attic, outside area and a garage if there is one. The attic should be dry and you should not be able to see any outside light coming in through the roof. It is always a good idea to see if there are any vents in the attic, although this is not as important as finding out if there are leaks. The attic should be insulated as well, this cuts down on lots of heat and help to keep the cool air inside if you run an air conditioner.

When renting a house you want everything to be up to standards so you will have an affordable place with all the things need to keep your energy bills down. You some place where you can be comfortable and relaxed in knowing everything is working correctly. If the house you are renting has central air, you want to inspect the unit to make sure it is not corroded or damaged.

Check the neighborhood. You want a safe neighborhood to live in and the only way to do this is by asking the property owner, who may not know or by calling the local police department. Walking through the neighborhood may also give you some clues. You might even see some of the neighbors outside and be able to ask questions.

The closest school and the transit system is another thing to ask about when renting a home. You want your children in a good school or if sending them to a different school, you need to know some information about the buses as well as how often they come through the neighborhood if they do at all in that area. Once you have answers to your important questions, it is always easier to make a decision if the place and area location is right for you.

Zero credit check loans for Tenant's

When searching for a loan it is guaranteed that borrowers are often going to be bombarded with the question, do you own a home? Lenders like homeowners because they have a great asset they can borrow against. Lenders know that homes and property go up in value as they age and that means they can get their money should the borrower default. What does this mean for the non-homeowner? Well, it does not have to hinder their efforts to get a loan because now there is an option cal...

When searching for a loan it is guaranteed that borrowers are often going to be bombarded with the question, do you own a home? Lenders like homeowners because they have a great asset they can borrow against. Lenders know that homes and property go up in value as they age and that means they can get their money should the borrower default. What does this mean for the non-homeowner? Well, it does not have to hinder their efforts to get a loan because now there is an option called a tenant loan.

A tenant loan is an unsecured loan meant for people who rent. They are especially designed for tenants who would otherwise have difficulty getting an unsecured loan. In the UK tenant loans are becoming quite popular. Lenders are seeing there is a large group of the population that does not own homes. They are seeing that they are losing out by focusing on only homeowners and that tenant loans are a booming business.

When getting a tenant loan or no credit check loan a borrower needs to still be careful. There are scams out there that can end up being very costly. One way to make sure to get a good deal is to shop around. Compare loans and find the most attractive offer. When comparing loans, though, borrowers should not forget to check out all of the terms and conditions. Sometimes extra expenses are hidden away and that could make what seems like a great loan turn out to be a bad choice.

Tenant loans can be used for many different purposes. They can be used for whatever the borrower wants. However, with an unsecured loan it is often easy to throw caution to the wind. That is not wise, though. An unsecured loan still must be paid back and even though the borrower has not risked any collateral, they still are risking a lot by frivolous taking out a loan without considering the cost or how they are going to pay it back. A tenant loan needs to be worked into the borrower's budget and paid back according to the agreement so the borrower does not end up in financial trouble.

When getting a tenant loan a borrower should be aware of their financial situation and make sure that a loan is the best option. It's not likely a lender will loan money to someone who can obviously not afford it, but sometimes financial troubles cannot be seen through comparing income statements and credit records. It is ultimately the borrower's responsibility to make sure they can afford the loan.

No credit check loans are a great way for someone to get a loan when they do not own a home or otherwise have collateral to secure a loan. However, it is still a loan. Lenders always regard unsecured loans as risky, even tenant loans. They will charge higher rates for this type of loan and may require a higher credit score. However, the availability of no credit check loans and the competition in the market is making them very desirable and a good idea for someone who needs a loan.

Landlord Mistakes

Classic business philosophy teaches that a great part of survival and subsequent success lies in an operation's ability to reduce mistakes. The cost of repairing the mistakes is inversely proportional to the amount of profit potential of the operation. In other words, "Mistakes Kill the Profit Margin" As landlord's, we don't want to do damage to the precious profit margin we fought so hard to nurture. A landlord's profit margin struggles every day to survive, grow and flourish in a sea of predators, competitors and government regulators. Below are the top 10 threats to you thriving profit margin.

Classic business philosophy teaches that a great part of survival and subsequent success lies in an operation's ability to reduce mistakes. The cost of repairing the mistakes is inversely proportional to the amount of profit potential of the operation. In other words..."Mistakes Kill the Profit Margin!!!!!"

As landlord's, we don't want to do damage to the precious profit margin we fought so hard to nurture. A landlord's profit margin struggles every day to survive, grow and flourish in a sea of predators, competitors and government regulators. Below are the top 10 threats to you thriving profit margin.

1-Poor Screening

The costliest mistake is accepting a new tenant without properly screening. An undesirable tenant will often have a poor rental and financial histories. Landlords should review previous landlord relations, credit reports, courthouse records and income. It is probable that if they have not met their obligations with previous landlords, then chances are that they will repeat their behavior with new landlords. Many landlords have faced horrific situations where tenants have stopped paying rent while employing legal maneuvering to avoid eviction. Others have faced tenants who moved in and initiated criminal activity, which adversely affected other tenants and neighbors. Either of these scenarios translates into expensive ordeals where the measures of rectifying the situation can threaten the financial stability of the landlord.

A thorough screening also involves verifying that the person who is applying is the same person that submits credit/criminal info for screening. A picture I.D. should be cross-referenced with the application. Landlords must make sure that there are no omissions, inaccuracies or inconsistency in the actual application. Due diligence will certainly save landlords much money and stress.

2-Lease Preparation

Having a poorly prepared lease is very costly because it is the document that legally binds the landlord to the tenant. It is the rules of the relationship that dictate conflict resolution, financial responsibility and terms of execution. Without a professionally prepared lease the landlord stands to forfeit many of the rights afforded to the owners of the property. Landlords need to employ leases that are designed to protect them and their property and not the other way around. Many generic leases do not take into account the values of the landlord. Therefore, a custom lease would assure the landlord that their interests are protected.

Many times landlords receive requests for agreements after the lease has been signed. Landlords will use their best judgment when deciding to agree to a proposal but must never neglect to put the agreement on paper. A verbal agreement is always vulnerable to a false interpretation by the tenant.

3-Rent Collections

Landlords must always enforce the terms of rent payment as it is written in the lease including late payments and fees. If not enforced, the landlord runs the risk of creating a dangerous precedent that will certainly cost the landlord dearly. If a tenant fails to pay rent for two weeks, then legal notices and actions must be initiated as soon as the law allows. Landlords should not accept partial payments. The courts interpret receiving partial payments from tenants as an acceptance of terms by the landlord. The eviction process is subsequently terminated for that rental period while landlord's costs increase.

If a tenant has had a poor history of paying rent on time, a landlord should consider not renewing the lease. Being late consistently is a sign of financial trouble and future uncertainty for the landlord. Poor payment habits can be a precursor to bankruptcy or evictions.

4-Law and Regulation Ignorance

Many landlords get into rental business without learning the rules of the game. To get a perspective of the folly of not knowing the rule, imagine trying to play basketball without knowledge of the rules. You would become paralyzed from the constant rule infractions. It would be impossible to win. Translated to the rental business: Knowledge of the Laws and regulations can make the difference between a profitable venture and a loser.

Landlords must familiarize themselves with the states' Landlord/Tenant Act. Every state has different laws, therefore due diligence must be taken by landlords to educate themselves. Landlords must also take the initiative to draw upon with the experiences of other landlords. Many landlord advocacy groups exist in most communities and the Internet.

Finally, it encouraged for landlords to develop a relationship with a real estate attorney that specializes in the rental industry. Having a knowledgeable supporter on your side can relieve a lot of uncertainty. A landlord must never wait to the last minute to develop a relationship with an attorney because the requirement of immediate response will prove to be costly.

5-Poor Response to Service Requests-

The number one reason that tenants do not renew their leases is poor response and execution for service requests from the landlord. Tenants expect a constant inspection, repair, and preservation of the general conditions of their rental home. This also includes a timely repair or replacement of parts for appliances. Everything has to be in working order and problems must be addressed quickly and courteously. Everything has to be in working order and problems must be addressed quickly and courteously. To facilitate an efficient delivery of maintenance requests, the property manager's best method of receiving these requests is actually answering the telephone. When the manager is too busy to actually answer the phone or the request comes at an odd hour, many properties utilize apartment call centers. This resource allows properties to always have a human responding to the needs of their tenants. The apartment call centers are industry specific and have a direct, open communication with the maintenance and property management. Maintenance requests should be supported by a shared calendar that documents the request cycle: creation, delivery, execution, completion and follow-up. Maintenance requests, if implemented properly, should be a team effort that will lessen and distribute workload through the property staff.

6-Not Employing Good Customer Service

Running a rental business is just like any other business in the sense with respect to employing good customer service. Many landlords forget that they would not be in business if it weren't for the customer. Practicing good customer service not only reduces tenant turnover, it also is one of the primary forms of marketing. Word of mouth advertising is the time tested, most effective way to promote any business. In the long run, a positive approach to communicating with your tenants will reflect in the profitability and value of a property. On the other hand, poor customer service will take a toll on the general conditions of the property. Tenants will not respect the property by not cleaning up after themselves or not following the property's rules and regulations. Therefore, poor customer service may result in high turnover, high vacancies, higher operational costs and lower profits.

7-Not paying taxes

Many landlords do not have their rental income as their primary source of income and neglect to report their income to the government. Others fail to pay property taxes because they don't reside in the property. Failing to declare income and ignoring property taxes can cause very expensive recovery efforts. The government will assess taxes, add fees, add penalties and assign interest. Other costs will come from attorney fees, added accountant charges and personal time. In extreme cases, landlords may get their property confiscated.

8-Not waiting for the funds to clear

In a rush to fill the occupancy, many landlords make the mistake of allowing the tenants to move in before the funds are cleared. The scenario of tenants moving into a property too soon has caused numerous headaches for landlords having to initiate eviction procedures without ever collecting any rent or deposit. Always ask for money orders and certified checks or simply wait for the funds to clear the bank.

9-Not conducting a detailed premove-in inspection

Neglecting to have the tenants complete a premove-in inspection can result in damages to a property that cannot be documented by the landlord. Payment for rent must not be accepted until this inspection is completed.

10-Not keeping a professional landlord/tenant relationship

Landlords must always uphold a professional relationship with tenants to avoid the pitfalls of not employing the codes of conduct that are based on the stipulations outlined in the lease. The professional relationship is based on the landlord realizing profits from the rental business. Changing the nature of the business relationship threatens the ability for the landlord to collect rent.

The psychology the Seller and the Tenant Buyer

What is in the minds of sellers and tenant buyers, and learning how to read them?

For those of you who were not psychology majors the "psyche" is someone's mind. What motivates them? What are they thinking? How can you better understand them? All of which is important to those of us in lease purchasing. In fact, it is important to any business person. The ability to know what motivates your customer, how your customer thinks, and tapping into their "psyche" is what makes some businesses successful and why others fail.

For those of us in lease purchasing when we make our calls we find out what motivates our sellers. We ask pointed questions to determine why they are selling their home. We build rapport with that seller. By the end of our telephone call we have an insight into what those particular sellers' wants and needs are.

Sometimes you need to educate the seller. For those of us in lease purchasing we can explain the various advantages of lease purchasing. The advantages we emphasize will be determined by that particular sellers' psyche. We can find out what is in a seller's psyche by how she or he has answered the questions that we have asked them. Their answers to our questions are what give us a pretty good feel for that seller.

In general, of course, a seller has a particular mind set. He or she wants to sell their home. They want to get a particular price for it. Their emotions are strong. They have very strong attachments to what they are selling, especially if they have lived there a long time. Depending on what their reasons for moving are: divorce, death in the family, birth of a child, job transfer, etc., remember they are going to be feeling certain things. Put yourself in their shoes. How would you feel if you were in their place?

If you cannot get inside the psyche of your seller you are not going to do deals. You must have empathy with the seller. Be a good listener. Ask questions and let the seller talk. This will give you the best insight into what the seller is thinking and what is motivating them.

While many of the above points are going to carry over into getting into the tenant buyers psyche there are also other considerations. You have to be able to understand what it is like to have credit problems, possibly a bankruptcy, medical problems, divorce, and a multitude of other bad things that might have happened to that tenant buyer. If you cannot relate to these issues, you will have a problem connecting with the tenant buyer's psyche.

Tenant buyers are looking at a dream. You have to feel that dream with them.

So to truly be successful in business you need to learn about the "psyche" of your customer. For those of us in lease purchasing that means the "psyche" of the seller and the tenant buyer

Tenant Options, options, and options within options

When searching for a loan it is guaranteed that borrowers are often going to be bombarded with the question, do you own a home? Lenders like homeowners because they have a great asset they can borrow against. Lenders know that homes and property go up in value as they age and that means they can get their money should the borrower default. What does this mean for the non-homeowner? Well, it does not have to hinder their efforts to get a loan because now there is an option called a tenant loan.

A tenant loan is an unsecured loan meant for people who rent. They are especially designed for tenants who would otherwise have difficulty getting an unsecured loan. In the UK tenant loans are becoming quite popular. Lenders are seeing there is a large group of the population that does not own homes. They are seeing that they are losing out by focusing on only homeowners and that tenant loans are a booming business.

When getting a tenant loan or no credit check loan a borrower needs to still be careful. There are scams out there that can end up being very costly. One way to make sure to get a good deal is to shop around. Compare loans and find the most attractive offer. When comparing loans, though, borrowers should not forget to check out all of the terms and conditions. Sometimes extra expenses are hidden away and that could make what seems like a great loan turn out to be a bad choice.

Tenant loans can be used for many different purposes. They can be used for whatever the borrower wants. However, with an unsecured loan it is often easy to throw caution to the wind. That is not wise, though. An unsecured loan still must be paid back and even though the borrower has not risked any collateral, they still are risking a lot by frivolous taking out a loan without considering the cost or how they are going to pay it back. A tenant loan needs to be worked into the borrower's budget and paid back according to the agreement so the borrower does not end up in financial trouble.

When getting a tenant loan a borrower should be aware of their financial situation and make sure that a loan is the best option. It's not likely a lender will loan money to someone who can obviously not afford it, but sometimes financial troubles cannot be seen through comparing income statements and credit records. It is ultimately the borrower's responsibility to make sure they can afford the loan.

No credit check loans are a great way for someone to get a loan when they do not own a home or otherwise have collateral to secure a loan. However, it is still a loan. Lenders always regard unsecured loans as risky, even tenant loans. They will charge higher rates for this type of loan and may require a higher credit score. However, the availability of no credit check loans and the competition in the market is making them very desirable and a good idea for someone who needs a loan.

Instant tenant loans

If you are a tenant or live at home with your family then you may already have experienced some problems when it comes to taking out a loan. Many of the great rates and deals that you see advertised are, quite literally, of no use to you at all as they may well be reserved for home/property owners. So, you can apply for them just to be turned down because you aren't a home owner or you might be given higher rates of interest than those advertised.

But, this is no reason to think that you can't find a loan to suit you and your budget – tenant loans may well be the perfect solution for your borrowing needs. As you might expect tenant loans are loans that are specially designed to serve the needs of tenants when they need to take out a loan.

So, you don't need to be a property owner to get a tenant loans and you don't need any form of security. All you need to do is to be willing to have the lender you approach check on your current finances and your past track record. Although, some tenant loans companies will even offer loans that don't need these financial checks – these may be a little more expensive, however.

You can take out tenant loans from various sources. In the past many big name lenders didn't used to like giving out loans to non property owners but the sector is a lot different nowadays. So, you can approach a big name bank or building society, for example, or you can simply approach a tenant loans specialist.

A lot of tenants do actually prefer to use a lender that only specializes in tenant loans nowadays. It can sometimes simply be quicker and easier to go down this path. And, many specialist tenant loans lenders will offer better rates of interest on the loans they give out because they have a better understanding of the sector that they specialize in as a whole.

Whether you approach a general lender or a specialist one for tenant loans you do need to make sure that you shop around for the best deal before you choose the loan that is right for you. There are hundreds of tenant loans on the sector right now and some of them really are a lot cheaper than others – especially if you can find them on the Internet – so do look for the one that will cost you as little as possible.

Unbelievable Opportunity... For Tenants Only

Good news for tenants! Now they can also access to loans market easily, as these days tenant loans are also available. For tenants, applying for a secured loan is not so easy. Since they do not possess any property thus they cannot use any thing as collateral against a secured loan. In such cases, tenant loan can be appropriate for them to finance their dreams.

As a sort of unsecured loans, tenant loans are available without any collateral. Thus a tenant easily can avail these loans. But the borrower's credit history and repayment capacity will be judged by the lender at the time of offering tenant loans.

But for availing a tenant loan, borrowers have to fulfill the following criteria:

Fulltime employment

A direct debit card acceptance facility should be attached with borrowers' bank account.

Presence of identification and residential proof.

And contact number- mobile or landline.

With tenant loans, a borrower can borrow anything from $1,000 to $50,000 along with a flexible repayment period of 1 to 25 years. Here, the reader should be aware that due to the absence of security, lenders charge high interest rate with tenant loans. But one can make the interest rate in his favor by negotiating. Even, if the borrower's credit history is good then he can avail these loans at flexible rate of interest.

Tenant loans can be used for various purposes like:

For consolidating debts....

Investing for property (own house or other real estate)

Making a holiday trip....

Repairing credit score....

Wedding purposes....

Buying new car and many more....

Seeming profitable...isn't it? But do remember that you will have to submit three years accommodation and address details and three years employment history along with a tenant loan application. Thus, if you change your abode or job recently, then you may have to face some hurdle at the time of availing a tenant loan.

At the same time, individuals are advised to check their repayment capacity at the time of availing a tenant loan. Still, the risk of collateral repossession is not attached with these loans, but in case of failing to repay the amount; lenders can jeopardize borrower's life by taking some legal steps.

Tenant loans are available for all sorts of tenants- council tenants, housing association tenants, MOD tenants, private landlord tenants, living with parents, housing executive tenant etc. These loans are providing them a chance to shape their dream and set it in the realm of reality.

Tenant Relocation Service

Many times when people move, they feel the need of using a relocation service. Most often, the people use the service because it will save them time and energy from doing all the hard work themselves.

What many people don't realize is that there are many different kinds of relocations service companies. In fact, one of the newest and more popular types of relocation service is a tenant relocation service. A tenant relocation service is a service that you may get when you are about to move in or out of an apartment or house; whichever is owned by a landlord. Many times people will use the tenant relocation service if they live in a big city or if they are pressed for time. However, some people use the tenant relocation service because it is easier for them; they don't have to deal with the mess of packing and boxing everything up!!

When a landlord rents out his or her property for rent, they may have in the rental agreement that a tenant relocation service is free. However, no all landlords will have that in the agreement. For many people, a tenant relocation service costs a lot of money; so many times they will have a stipulation that the relocation service is for only if you move in the same town or a certain amount of miles.

Other than just packing and unpacking a person's items, some tenant relocation service will include setting up the all the appliances to the furniture. However, that is one thing that you will have to check with the company that you choose. Many times if the tenant relocation service does not come with the setting up of the furniture and appliances, you may have it added for a few more dollars.

One thing that is great about having a tenant relocation service is that in most cases, you the tenant, will be able to choose which relocation service it is that you want to use. In most cases, it would not hurt to look around at all the available companies. Many times because they sound good, does not mean that they are. In fact, the best thing that you can do for yourself and your possessions is to interview some of the surrounding companies; that way you can find out which ones seem to be the best and will take care of your things. Many times people will go on the internet to look for some relocation service companies, if they can't find any in their area. Also, they can interview the companies through email, rather than trying to get a hold of them over the phone! If you cannot choose a company of your choice, you can either hope that your things make it in one piece, or you can hire a company that you trust!

Just because there are many tenant relocation service companies around, does not mean that they are what you need. In fact, many people will opt on having a relocation service because they either don't trust them, or that they want to do the packing themselves.

Tax time for rental investors

While owning a rental property can be a terrific way to bring in income, those extra dollars can make things complicated when it comes to preparing a tax return.

Fortunately for the 15 million people who own rental properties in the U.S., there are ways to make tax season a little more manageable:

Store your receipts, bills and statements during the year. This will make it much easier to locate and organize them at tax time. Create an envelope or folder for each property, and put all of your receipts in there during the year. Do the same for regular bills such as the mortgage, property taxes, insurance, utilities, etc.

Keep good rental payment records. You probably get a lot of checks-and even cash-from your tenants during the year. It can be really hard to figure out at tax time if you don't stay organized during the year.

Know what property each check comes from. You can record this with your bank deposits in your checkbook or spreadsheet or rental property software.

Use rental property software like Quicken Rental Property Manager 2.0, designed for people who own up to 10 properties and 25 total units. It makes it easier to file taxes and manage rental property income and expenses. This can help eliminate hours at the end of the year preparing for that Schedule E. Using the software, you can simply print the tax report and transfer the data to the form, give it to your accountant, or export data directly to tax preparation software like TurboTax.

Separate security deposits from rent payments. Security deposits are not considered income if you intend to return them to the tenant, so make sure these deposits are separated from rent payments. Flag expense receipts. Some expenses are hard to classify properly for the IRS. When you replace the faucet in the bathroom, is that considered a repair or a capital improvement? It makes a big difference to Uncle Sam because 100 percent of repairs can be deducted this year, but capital improvements must be deducted over time. When you're not sure, flag those receipts so you can later discuss them with your accountant. Keep them in a separate place or flag them in your expense journal. Lastly, don't forget the mileage deduction. You probably rack up a lot of miles driving to and from your properties and those trips to the hardware store. It can be tedious to keep track of the mileage, but it really pays off since the IRS allows you to deduct about 45 cents/mile. To make it easier, use an Internet map ser-vice such as MapQuest to look up the mileage for common trips-like between your home and each property.

Sharing a Rental with a Roommate

There are a lot of great benefits to sharing a rental with a roommate, like sharing the cost of rent and utilities. There could potentially be downsides of having a roommate if careful planning is not taken when choosing a roommate. There are agreements that need to be made prior to sharing a space, and knowing the legalities of sharing a space is necessary. Taking certain precautions will save two or more a lot of heart ache in the future.

When two or more people sign the same rental agreement or lease, or enter into the same oral rental agreement, they are cotenants and share the same legal rights and responsibilities. This - legal principle, known as **joint and several liabilities**, has enormous implications for cotenants.

This is referring to housemates who are cotenants, not tenant and subtenant. There are important distinctions between the two. A tenant and her/her subtenant, for example, someone who has sublet an apartment from you and has not signed the lease or rental agreement, do not share the same rights and responsibilities with respect to each other or to the landlord.

What is a cotenant? A cotenant is one of two or more tenants holding title to the same property.

What is a subtenant? A subtenant is a person who rents land, a house, or the like from a tenant.

How to Choose a Roommate

When choosing a roommate, try to choose someone that is somewhat like you. If you are a very calm person, why would you choose a roommate that is wild and crazy? If you are a person with clean habits, why would you choose a roommate that does not have clean habits. It would be to your advantage to choose someone that you already know. Friends and family members are good first choices. Choose people that you know are responsible enough to handle the responsibilities that come with being a cotenant. If family and friends are not prospects, then talk with them anyway to see if they know of anyone that may want to rent a space. Lastly if those options still do not work. You must place ads in community papers or on community boards. You could briefly put in that ad what you are looking for in a roommate.

Get references before making a final decision. The steps to find a compatible roommate are much like those for choosing a reliable employee. A good word from past roommates and landlords can help give you a brighter picture of the candidate's personality. Since you are relying on this person to share bills, a credit check might also be in order.

Interview prospective candidates in person. The convenience of emails and phone contact may seem quicker but, it is essential that you sit down face to face. That way, you get a sense of how comfortable you would feel seeing that person every day. Allow that person to do most of the talking. In other words do not start out allowing that person to know the things that you do or do not want. Just allow him or her to tell you a little about themselves so that you can get a feel of who that person is. You could ask them questions about smoking habits, cleaning habits, or questions about friends that they would invite into the home or apartment. If there are things you feel you may forget, write them down on paper, and do not be afraid to use that piece of paper while interviewing.

Roommate Agreements

When you choose your roommate it is vital that you have a roommate agreement. When two people or more live under the same roof disagreements are bound to happen.

A roommate agreement is a written document that defines the obligations and rights of two or more people who share housing. These agreements are not the same as rental agreements, leases or a sub-leases, which primarily address financial and maintenance responsibilities between landlord and tenant or a tenant and his sub-leaser. Instead, a roommate agreement often deals with issues unique to unrelated people living together, such as rules about having overnight guests or performing chores in addition to financial arrangements. By having a written, signed agreement, you and your roommates can avoid misunderstandings and conflict.

What Are The Legal Responsibilities of a Roommate Or a Cotenant?

When all the roommates of a rental property are listed in the lease, each is responsible for the entire amount of rent due to the landlord. If the roommate is not named on the lease and has not signed the lease, the roommate usually pays his portion of the rent to the named tenant, who then pays the landlord. This tenant is responsible for the full amount of rent. Roommates become co-tenants when they simultaneously sign a lease. They share the same legal rights and responsibilities.

How Do I Add a Roommate To a Lease?

In order to establish tenancy, most states require that the new roommate have the consent of the landlord and that the roommate contribute to or pay rent.

To gain the landlord's consent, consider the occupancy limits of the apartment as well as any behavioral requirements the landlord may have. Credit history, employment history, rental history and any other background check may be conducted.

Rent law for new tenants is subject to the responsibilities listed above. Expect rent and security deposits to go up as well.

Disputes between Roommates

Informal arrangements are made between roommates all the time, about rent, bedrooms, or any other issues. Disputes between roommates are bound to arise. To protect yourself, it may be best to prepare for any disagreements that are likely to happen. The first step is to choose your roommates carefully. Before renting, make sure you and your roommates discuss important issues such as how much of the rent you each pay, what spaces in the property each will occupy, chores, food, and moving out. These arrangements can and should be put in writing. Courts will enforce rent-sharing agreements among cotenants.

What Happens If One Roommate Doesn't Pay Rent?

The splitting up of rent among cotenants does not affect the landlord. The landlord must still be paid no matter who pays him. The amount of rent each tenant pays is up to the roommates. Each is still equally liable to the landlord for the full amount of the rent. If one roommate does not pay the rent, for whatever reason, the remaining roommates are still responsible for paying the full amount.

What Happens If One Roommate Decides to Leave?

A cotenant who decides to leave before the term of the tenancy is over is still liable. Before leaving, the cotenant should obtain the consent of the landlord because if he does not the landlord may evict everyone else. Usually, a landlord will not evict the other roommates unless they cannot show that they will be able to pay the rent without the departing roommate. If your roommate is departing, try to create an agreement by which you set out the amount of rent that he will pay. If the cotenant refuses to pay rent you can bring a lawsuit against him/her.

Can a Roommate be evicted?

Joint tenants cannot be evicted by their fellow tenants because their contract is with the landlord. Subtenant eviction will differ by state. Some states treat the tenant as a landlord in relation to the subtenant. Other states will not permit tenants to evict their subtenants without the landlord.

The landlord has the power to evict any of the roommates, regardless of their status. The landlord has the power to evict all the roommates but may reverse the evictions of certain tenants under certain conditions which vary by state.

All evictions made must be legal: A person cannot evict a tenant without a prior notice that must be given and a court order must be given to have the police remove the tenants. To remove a tenant any other way is illegal.

Can a Landlord Reject a Roommate?

The landlord reserves the right to reject any tenants. It is important for the landlord, however, not to treat the person as a tenant. This means that if the landlord accepts any type of payment, checks, cash or even services, the person may automatically become a tenant in the eyes of the law.

A landlord who wishes to avoid this should not treat the person as a tenant in anyway and instead order the person to leave or face trespassing charges.

Do I Need A Lawyer for my Roommate/Co-Tenant Problem?

Sometimes serious disputes can arise between roommates or co-tenants. An experienced property attorney can help you decide whether or not to sue your roommate or cotenant. If you need to go to court, a property attorney can represent you and help you get the best results possible.

Playing It Fair With Your Roommate

1. **Communication is Key!** It is very important to live with people you can talk to easily. Whether you want to have a really close relationship with them or not, you still need to be able to tell them when you are not happy or if you disagree with something that is going on.

2. **Decide who is Responsible for What:** Often with two roommates it is easy to give and take the shared household duties. Living in a household of three may be different because someone usually is doing more than the other two. Even if this means making a chart listing all of the household chores with the days of the week that each tenant should do their chores, and using a magnet to put the list on the refrigerator, then I suggest doing whatever you must do to keep peace in the home.

3. **Split the Bills Equally:** If you have cable, internet, phone, electric, water and gas to share, it's easiest just to split the bills equally. One person might use more of the electricity and never use the gas, but sometimes trying to calculate who uses more of what just gets complicated, especially when most people are not even at home at the same time. If you can move in knowing everything is split evenly it makes collecting money a lot easier each month. Also if you are the sole name on all the bills you will find it even more frustrating trying to collect down to the nearest dollar.

4. **Respect Each Other's Privacy:** This probably seems like an obvious statement, but you would be surprised what boundaries are crossed when people live together. Remember to knock first. Remember not everyone is a morning person. Try to be mindful of overnight guests. How loud should I play my music and when? Always ask before borrowing, no matter how close you are. Your visitors should also respect your roommate. Visitors should not be allowed to stay the night often because sometimes the other roommate will start feeling that they should not have to split the bills in half if there is a guess in the home spending the night all the time and not paying anything.

5. **Put a Lock on Your Door:** If you are not sure about your roommate or your roommate's friends, I think it would be safe to put a lock on your bedroom door. If you are in a home with

three or four people, who all work different schedules, all with different friends, you never knows what is going on when you are at work or away for long periods of time.

6. **Common Annoyances between Roommates:** 1. Do your own dishes. You ate off them, you should do them. If one roommate mandates they be done right after eating, this is a respect issue and everyone should abide by it. 2. Same goes for taking out the trash- if it's piling up just take it out, don't wait for someone to assume responsibility of it. Each tenant should be very clean 3. Sharing the bathroom can always be a challenge. Sometimes a verbal agreement or schedule is nice, especially if you both work the same hours.

7. **Pets:** Whether you're moving into a home with existing pets, or if you're bringing yours with you, it's important to establish the responsibility. Can you depend on your roommate to feed your dog if you stay out late? Do you want to be stuck cleaning the litter box of your roommate's cat? All these are valid concerns that need to be addressed early on.

Rental Commercial Property

A commercial lease should clearly define the space that the tenant will be leasing. Leases typically include both a street address and a site plan showing the demised premises, and set for the square footage of the demised premises. A demised premise refers to the space occupied by a tenant under a lease contract. The lease contract requires careful reading because it usually includes the responsibilities between the landlord and tenant surrounding the care of the demised premises.

Make sure the lease clearly defines the demised premises, and that the demised premises described in the lease matches the demised premises you are expecting to receive. Also, make sure that your demised premise has sufficient parking spaces and sign rights to allow you to operate your business.

Is This a Gross Lease or a Net Lease? A commercial lease should tell you what is included in the rental amount that you pay the landlord. Most leases are gross leases, triple net leases, or fall somewhere in between. Unfortunately, not all leases will state explicitly into which category they fall, so you need to read the lease carefully. A gross lease typically is all-inclusive, meaning that the tenant pays the landlord one sum and the landlord is responsible for payment of real estate taxes, insurance and maintenance expenses. Tenant utilities may or may not be included within a gross lease. In a triple net lease, the tenant pays a set rental amount to the landlord, but also pays a share of the landlord's real estate taxes, insurance, maintenance expenses, and building utilities. Understanding the difference between a gross and triple net lease is particularly important when comparing multiple spaces because it helps to ensure you are comparing apples to apples.

How is My Rental Rate Determined? A commercial lease should clearly define what your rental rate will be for the entire term of the lease. Generally, this is done through a rental chart which states the annual rental rate for each year of the lease and what the tenant's equal monthly payments will be based on the corresponding annual rate. In most leases, the annual rental rate increases from year to year either by a flat amount of 2.5% or by reference to an exterior formula in proportion to increases in the cost of living allowance. In some retail leases, the tenant is responsible for paying the annual rental amount plus a percentage of the tenant's sales for the year, which is known as percentage rent.

What is Included in Your CAM? A triple net commercial lease should state the amount, if any, the tenant must contribute toward (common area maintenance) expenses, or CAM. CAM may include costs of snow removal, security, parking attendants, building maintenance, building management fees, etc. The simplest method for determining a tenant's share of CAM is to divide the number of square feet in the tenant's space by the total number of rentable square feet in the office building or shopping center. Of course, commercial leases do not always handle things in the simplest manner, so CAM allocation should be reviewed carefully.

What Can You Do in Your Demised Premises? A commercial lease likely will tell you what you can and cannot do in your demised premises. Office leases often state that the space will be used for general office use and for no other purpose. Retail spaces often get more specific. Further, you need to know whether your lease includes an exclusive, which is a provision that gives you the exclusive right to operate your type of business in the building or shopping center. Exclusives are the reason that you rarely see competing beauty salons in the same shopping plaza.

Who Pays For Repairs? A commercial lease should clearly define who is responsible for repairs of the demised premises, the building, the parking lot and the core building systems (plumbing, electric, HVAC, etc.). The question here is not who pays for the repairs, but who is responsible for making sure the repairs are made in the first place. Commercial tenants often maintain the demised premises and any core building systems to the extent they are located within the demised premises, while the landlord maintains everything else.

Will There Be a Build-out And, If So, Who Pays For It? Commercial space tends to be rather generic and may require modifications, or a (build-out), for use by a particular tenant. Accordingly, a commercial lease often states whether the landlord or the tenant will make improvements to the demised premises to get ready for the tenant's occupancy. When the landlord pays for the improvements, the amount spent by the landlord is called an allowance. If improvements are needed, the lease must clearly state what improvements will be made, who will complete the improvements, when the improvements will be complete, and the amount of any allowance.

The foregoing list should provide some guidance when reviewing your commercial lease, but the list is by no means exhaustive. Commercial leases typically deal with a host of other issues as well, including the length of the lease, tenant extension or renewal, the tenant's ability to assign the lease or sublet the demised premises, what constitutes a default and what remedies are available for a default, tenant insurance obligations, environmental contamination, etc. These are all important issues and must be reviewed carefully and understood by the tenant.

Setting Rental Rates

Supply

How many properties are there like yours on the market? If there are lot of vacancies around, your property will have a lot of competition.

Demand

Is your area hot? Does the area have good schools? Great local features such as beaches, parks, mountains, tourist attractions, etc? Are there any nice amenities? Remember popular areas, amenities, or local features draw tenants and are great for rent prices.

Your Interests

What are your goals? Are you looking to rent the property out quickly? Are you looking to rent the property for one of the lowest rates? Are you looking for the largest amount of potential tenants to choose from?

Scope out the Competition

It is important that you think about your specific property and how it compares to other rentals. Look at all the features your property has as compared to what other properties have. You should look at what each property has and do a realistic comparison. It is also a good idea to check the nightly rates for hotels in your area. Next to other vacation homes, hotels are your biggest competitor.

List your property too high, and you it will be very hard for you to find a renter. If you your property too low, then you risk losing out on thousands of dollars over the course of your tenant's residency. It's a delicate balance that you must strike, but once you do, price will no longer be an issue that prevents you from renting your place.

Need some advice on choosing the right price tag? Here are some tips that may help you settle on the right number, and even help you understand why.

Do Some Online Homework

There are a multitude of websites that offer rental rate suggestions and you should investigate as many of them as you can. Choose at least three sites that offer estimation capabilities and compare their suggestions on you should price your rental. Try visiting this website. (HUDUser.org) The U.S. Department of Housing and Urban Development's official website. They will be able to offer the most objective estimation of rental prices in your area.

After you have gathered numbers from multiple sources, average all of the prices together. This will give you an idea of a figure to work from, and you can use it set an asking range.

Compare the Virtual to the Actual

Now that you've got an idea of what you think your rate should be, compare the figure to actual rental rates in your area. Check in with the owners of condo rentals and apartment complexes in your neighborhood and ask for quotes on a unit similar to the ones you're renting. You can also browse Craigslist or check the classifieds for rental properties similar to yours. Remember to take the information you gather and decide whether you should adjust your original figure.

Do a Test Run

List your unit with Craigslist, or another free advertising venue with what you think is the fair and ideal rental price. If you get a few bites, then you're probably within a reasonable range. If your property gains little or no attention, chances are pretty good that you have overpriced yourself. You should consider changing your rate.

Make sure all your questions have been answered and you know exactly what you are getting into. Visit MrLandlord.com for useful information on rental success.

Financing Options for Rental Property

Mortgage: Mortgage from a bank is a feasible option for a person who is able and willing to fund between 20% and 30% of the value of the property. People who are able to fund up to 30% of the property's worth get the best deal on interest rates. The reason why banks require a down payment for purchasing the rental property is because they consider it a risky investment. A person is likely to default on the rental property mortgage payment than a mortgage payment on his home. A person needs to have a really good credit score in order to borrow from the bank. In the present scenario, a credit score in the range of 700 - 750 can get a person a really good deal on the mortgage.

Seller Financing: This is an option for a person who would prefer paying a down payment of about 10% of the value of the property. The seller can then finance another 10%. The remaining 80% is financed by taking a mortgage from a bank. A seller might be willing to finance the deal because financing provides him the flexibility of deciding when to sell the house or how long to occupy the house before vacating it. The seller gets a greater return from this investment as opposed to the return he can hope to get by investing in a (certificate of deposit). The buyer benefits because the seller charges a low rate of interest as compared to the bank and allows him to pay only interest for sixty months. At the end of sixty months, the buyer pays a lump sum amount as a balloon payment.

Rehabilitation Loan: Rehabilitation loans are a must in case of buying a foreclosure. The loan, as the name suggests, is used for reconstruction, and is generally provided for a period of six months by the rehab lender which is also called a private lender. The borrower can extend the loan on a monthly basis for up to thirteen months. The lender will generally provide up to 70% of the after repair value of the house or 95% of the cost of the reconstruction project.

A person would have to have to consult an attorney and get the necessary papers ready, and negotiate on the price with the seller. One also needs to look for tenants and decide on how to manage the property. A property manager can be hired to take care of the property or a person may choose to manage it himself. There is a number of property management software available in the market, the use of which will definitely aid the process of rental property management.

www.ingramcontent.com/pod-product-compliance
Lightning Source LLC
Chambersburg PA
CBHW081603170526
45166CB00009B/2811